PEOPLE WHO

LOVE TO EAT ARE ALWAYS

THE BEST PEOPLE

Julia Child

PEOPLE WHO LOVE TO EAT ARE ALWAYS THE BEST PEOPLE

AND OTHER WISDOM

ALFRED A. KNOPF

NEW YORK 2020

THIS IS A BORZOI BOOK
PUBLISHED BY ALFRED A. KNOPF

Copyright © 2020 by The Julia Child Foundation for Gastronomy
and the Culinary Arts

Illustrations by Sidonie Coryn
Edited by Lexy Bloom, Tom Pold, and Todd Schulkin

LIBRARY OF CONGRESS CATALOGING-IN-PUBLICATION DATA
Names: Child, Julia, author.
Title: People who love to eat are always the best people : and other
wisdom / Julia Child.
Description: New York : Alfred A. Knopf, 2020.
Identifiers: LCCN 2020005031 (print) | LCCN 2020005032 (ebook) |
ISBN 9780525658795 (hardcover) | ISBN 9780525658801 (ebook)
Subjects: LCSH: Child, Julia. | Cooks—United States—Quotations.
Classification: LCC TX649.C47 A25 2020 (print) | LCC TX649.C47 (ebook)
| DDC 641.5092 [B]—dc23
LC record available at https://lccn.loc.gov/2020005031
LC ebook record available at https://lccn.loc.gov/2020005032

Jacket illustration and design by Joan Wong
Author photograph by Paul Child © The Julia Child Foundation
for Gastronomy and the Culinary Arts

Manufactured in Canada
First Edition

A NOTE ON THE QUOTES

We at The Julia Child Foundation for Gastronomy and the Culinary Arts have learned that people love to quote Julia. Julia herself certainly loved to quip. She was even known to quote herself, sometimes changing her words just enough to leave the "original" to each person's memory. Such is the public affection and fascination with all things Julia that stories about things she never did or said are frequently told with conviction. Given all the lore, we felt it was time to gather Julia's wisdom into an authoritative compendium. We hope you enjoy her enduring wit as much as we still do.

PEOPLE WHO

LOVE TO EAT ARE ALWAYS

THE BEST PEOPLE

Learn to cook—try new recipes,
learn from your mistakes, be fearless,
and above all have fun!

Food, like the people who eat it,
can be stimulated by wine or spirits.
And, as with people, it can also
be spoiled.

You can always judge the quality of a cook or restaurant by roast chicken. While it does not require years of training to produce a juicy, brown, buttery, crisp-skinned, heavenly bird, it does entail such a greed for perfection that one is under compulsion to hover over the bird, listen to it, above all see that it is continually basted, and that it is done just to the proper turn.

NO ONE IS BORN

A GREAT COOK,

ONE LEARNS

BY DOING.

I think careful cooking is love, don't you?
The loveliest thing you can cook for someone
who's close to you is about as nice a
Valentine as you can give.

DON'T FORGET
THE *butter*—
THE FRENCH
NEVER DO!

* * * * * * * *

* * * * * * * *

Certainly one of the important requirements for learning how to cook is that you also learn how to eat. If you don't know how an especially fine dish is supposed to taste, how can you produce it? Just like becoming an expert in wine—you learn by drinking it, the best you can afford—you learn about great food by finding the best there is, whether simple or luxurious. Then you savor it, analyze it, and discuss it with your companions, and you compare it with other experiences.

FIND SOMETHING YOU'RE
PASSIONATE ABOUT
AND KEEP TREMENDOUSLY
INTERESTED IN IT.

It is hard to imagine a civilization without onions; in one form or another their flavor blends into almost everything in the meal except the dessert.

Theoretically a good cook should be
able to perform under any circumstances,
but cooking is much easier, pleasanter, and
more efficient if you have the right tools.

Therein lies the science of the experienced wine connoisseur—the more you drink (and think upon it), the more you'll know.

[COOKING] TAKES ALL
OF YOUR INTELLIGENCE
AND ALL OF YOUR DEXTERITY.
IT'S ALWAYS CREATIVE,
IT'S ALWAYS NEW,
IT'S ALWAYS FUN.

The sweetness and generosity and politeness
and gentleness and humanity of the French
had shown me how lovely life can be
if one takes time to be friendly.

TEACHING SHOULD
NEVER BE DULL,
EVEN IF YOU'RE TALKING
ABOUT HOW TO RAISE
TURNIPS IN DENMARK.

The soufflé is the egg at its most magnificent.
How glorious it is when borne to the table,
its head rising dramatically out of its dish,
and swaying voluptuously
as it is set down.

SERIOUS ARTIST OR

WEEKEND AMATEUR,

IT'S MORE FUN COOKING

for COMPANY

in COMPANY.

The pleasures of the table—that lovely old-fashioned phrase—depict food as an art form, as a delightful part of civilized life. In spite of food fads, fitness programs, and health concerns, we must never lose sight of a beautifully conceived meal.

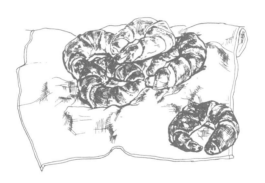

How I love to come back to this sweet
and natural France, this warmth,
these wonderful smells, this graciousness
and coziness and freedom of spirit.

I THINK
EVERY WOMAN
SHOULD HAVE
A BLOWTORCH.

B.T.F.P.—Before The Food Processor—it was only
the practiced cook who produced decent pastry
dough. And what a to-do it was: first the making of
a fountain of flour on a clean board, the clearing
of a space in its center for the butter and liquids,
and the working of them together with cool,
deft fingers—all done by that practiced cook
with an infuriatingly calm smile of superiority.
Now, in less than five minutes, that wonderful
F.P. machine enables any one of us to make perfect
pastry dough every time. We are thus, with our
own triumphant smiles, instantly masters of
the quiche, the tart, the turnover, countless
hors d'oeuvre niblets, to say nothing of the
chicken pot pie.

GOOD FOOD IS
ALWAYS ENHANCED BY
ITS AMBIENCE.

All of the techniques employed
in French cooking are aimed at one goal:
How does it taste?

If you have not a good wine to use,
it is far better to omit it, for a poor one
can spoil a simple dish and utterly
debase a noble one.

Wallop your steaks! Whoosh up your egg whites! And, behind your chafing dish and before your guests, act with assurance and decisiveness.

I WAS THIRTY-NINE

WHEN I STARTED COOKING;

UP UNTIL THEN,

I JUST ATE.

A fine loaf of plain French bread, the long crackly kind a Frenchman tucks under his arm as he hurries home to the family lunch, has a very special quality. Its inside is patterned with holes almost like Swiss cheese, and when you tear off a piece it wants to come sideways; it has body, chewability, and tastes and smells of the grain.

The only time to eat diet food
is while you're waiting for
the steak to cook.

I'M A

BEET

FREAK.

True cooks love to set one flavor against another in the imagination, to experiment with the great wealth of fresh produce in the supermarkets, to bake what previously they braised, to try new devices. We all have flops, of course, but we learn from them; and, when an invention or variation works out at last, it is an enormous pleasure to propose it to our fellows.

Let's all play with our food, I say, and, in so doing, let us advance the state of the art together.

An American meat loaf
is for all the world a French pâté
minus the wine and truffles.

Remember, "No one's more important than people"! In other words, friendship is the most important thing—not career or housework, or one's fatigue—and it needs to be tended and nurtured.

I began to notice cats everywhere, lurking in alleys or sunning themselves on walls or peering down at you from windows. They were such interesting, independent-minded creatures. I began to equate them with Paris.

It is probably really much better not to see
one's intimate family for more than
two and a half days at a time.

I MUST SAY,

I DO LOVE FRENCH PEOPLE,

AND HAD NO IDEA THEY

WOULD BE AS THEY ARE.

Writing is hard work. It did not always come easily for me, but once I got going on a subject, it flowed. Like teaching, writing has to be lively, especially for things as technical and potentially dullsville as recipes. I tried to keep my style amusing and non-pedantic, but also clear and correct. I remained my own best audience: I wanted to know why things happened on the stove, and when, and what I could do to shape the outcome. And I assumed that our ideal reader—the servantless American cook who enjoyed producing something wonderful to eat—would feel the same way.

You don't have to cook fancy or
complicated masterpieces—just good food
from fresh ingredients.

I'VE LIVED IN A LOT
OF PLACES . . . AFTER
A WHILE YOU DECIDE THAT
YOU CAN HAVE YOUR
OWN OPINIONS.

A pot saver is a self-hampering cook.
Use all the pans, bowls, and equipment
you need, but soak them in water
as soon as you are through with them.

Dining with one's friends and beloved family is certainly one of life's primal and most innocent delights, one that is both soul-satisfying and eternal.

I closed my eyes and inhaled the rising perfume. Then I lifted a forkful of fish to my mouth, took a bite, and chewed slowly. The flesh of the sole was delicate, with a light but distinct taste of the ocean that blended marvelously with the browned butter. I chewed slowly and swallowed. It was a morsel of perfection . . . It was the most exciting meal of my life.

If you don't eat with gusto, the gastric juices
are not going to work properly . . . You just
won't digest your food properly.
So don't eat meekly!

THE MEMORY OF A
GOOD FRENCH *pâté*
CAN HAUNT YOU
FOR YEARS.

* * ** * ** *

* * ** * * * *

My, the things I've cheapened by
using fat instead of butter,
or this instead of that, all for
a few cents of economy.

A COOKBOOK IS

ONLY AS GOOD AS ITS

POOREST RECIPE.

FAT GIVES THINGS FLAVOR.

Drama is very important in life:
You have to come on with a bang.
You never want to go out with a whimper.
Everything can have drama if it's
done right. Even a pancake.

I'M NOT A CHEF;
I'M A TEACHER
AND A COOK.

The lamplit city glittered in its puddles,
and Notre Dame loomed out of the mist,
giving our nerves a twinge. When you know
your time in a place is running out,
you try to fix such moments
in your mind's eye.

I say fie to those oenophilic spoilsports who insist that wine goes with neither eggs nor salads. Wine is essential with anything! Particularly omelettes for lunch.

Cooking is not a particularly difficult art,
and the more you cook and learn about cooking,
the more sense it makes. But like any art it
requires practice and experience. The most
important ingredient you can bring to it is
love of cooking for its own sake.

IF YOU'RE
AFRAID OF BUTTER,
USE CREAM.

When you are the cook in the family,
plan your vegetables ahead so that you will
have leftovers for soup; it will save you a
great deal of time, and make you feel
remarkably clever besides.

One of the secrets of cooking is
to learn to correct something if you can,
and bear with it if you cannot.

* * * * * * * *

* * * * * * * *

THE PLEASURES

OF THE TABLE

ARE INFINITE.

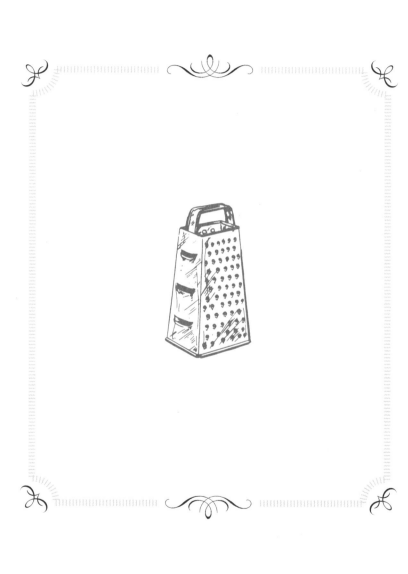

To be a good cook
you have to have a love of the good,
a love of hard work,
and a love of creating.

You can save a tremendous
amount of time, and also derive
a modest pride, in learning how
to use a knife professionally.

EATING IS ONE
OF THE FRENCH
NATIONAL SPORTS.

What a beautiful, appetizing, and
satisfying creation the salad is—and what
a simple one, too. Nature provides;
you combine.

WITHOUT PEANUTS

IT ISN'T A

COCKTAIL PARTY.

There are few things more satisfying to the soul
than the look and smell of a French *charcuterie*.

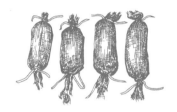

There is hardly a man alive who does not adore soup, particularly when it is homemade. Hot soup on a cold day, cold soup on a hot day, and the smell of soup simmering in the kitchen are fundamental, undoubtedly even atavistic, pleasures and solaces that give a special kind of satisfaction.

I wondered if the nation's gastronomical lust
had its roots not in the sunshine of art
but in the deep, dark deprivations
France had suffered over the centuries.

* * ** * ** *

* * ** * ** *

Maybe the cat has fallen into the stew,
or the lettuce has frozen, or the cake has
collapsed—*eh bien, tant pis!*

Usually one's cooking is better than one thinks
it is. And if the food is truly vile, as my ersatz
eggs Florentine surely were, then the cook
must simply grit her teeth and bear it with a
smile—and learn from her mistakes.

Dieters are the best audience
a cook ever has, for they savor and
remember every morsel.

The more you know,
the more you can create.
There's no end to imagination
in the kitchen.

A chicken should taste like chicken
and be so good in itself that it is an
absolute delight to eat as a perfectly plain,
buttery roast, sauté, or grill.

People who love to eat are always
the best people.

Immersed in cookery, I found that deeply
sunk childhood memories had begun to
bubble up to the surface. Recollections of the
pleasant-but-basic cooking of our hired cooks
in Pasadena came back to me—the big hams
or gray roast beef served with buttery mashed
potatoes. But then, unexpectedly, so did yet
deeper memories of more elegant meals prepared
in a grand manner by accomplished cooks when
I was just a girl—such as wonderfully delicate and
sauced fish. As a child I had barely noticed these
real cooks, but now their faces and their food
suddenly came back to me in vivid detail.
Funny how memory works.

I think one of the terrible things today
is that people have this deathly fear of food:
fear of eggs, say, or fear of butter.
Most doctors feel you can have a little
bit of everything.

Any *cassoulet* worthy of the name is not a light dish, and is probably best served as a noontime dinner.

If pie dough has always been your
culinary bugaboo, remember that no one
is born a pastry chef, everyone has had to learn,
and that the first big step is to make the decision
that you are now, today, going to learn to make
a decent pie crust. Then make pie dough
every day or two for a week or more; serve
everything you can think of in pastry.

I JUST HATE

HEALTH FOOD.

Any cook or housewife is well advised
to learn as much as possible about grades
and cuts of beef, as a vague beef-buyer
is open to countless unnecessary
disappointments and expenses.

NO MATTER WHAT

HAPPENS IN THE KITCHEN,

NEVER APOLOGIZE.

Some children like to make castles out of their rice pudding, or faces with raisins for eyes. It is forbidden—so sternly that, when they grow up, they take a horrid revenge by dyeing meringues pale blue or baking birthday cakes in the form of horseshoes or lyres or whatnot. That is not playing with food, that is trifling.

"Play" to me means freedom and delight, as in the phrase "play of imagination."

Always remember: If you're alone in
the kitchen and you drop the lamb,
you can always just pick it up.
Who's going to know?

Anyone who has eaten a plateful of small, tender, fresh, green peas in Italy or France in the springtime is not likely to forget the experience.

A sauce should not be considered a disguise or a mask; its role is to point up, to prolong, or to complement the taste of the food it accompanies, or to contrast with it, or to give variety to its mode of presentation.

I felt a lift of pure happiness every time
I looked out the window. I had come to the
conclusion that I must really *be* French,
only no one had ever informed me of this fact.
I loved the people, the food, the lay of the land,
the civilized atmosphere, and the
generous pace of life.

When you buy vegetables fresh and cook them lovingly, you may find yourself more renowned for your remarkable zucchini stuffed with almonds than for your spectacular *crêpes Suzette.*

Toujours bon appétit!

A NOTE ON SOURCES

The quotations in this book, listed by the pages on which they appear, are taken from the following sources.

BOOKS WRITTEN BY JULIA CHILD

PAGES 3 AND 9 *From Julia Child's Kitchen*

PAGES 5, 7, 15, 19, 21, 22, 37, 39, 63, 71, 87, 93, 97, 115, 123, 128, 135, AND 137 *Mastering the Art of French Cooking, Volume I* (with Louisette Bertholle and Simone Beck)

PAGES 24, 53, 54, 59, 67, 83, 107, 109, 119, 139, AND 143 *My Life in France* (with Alex Prud'homme)

PAGE 26 *Julia's Kitchen Wisdom*

PAGE 27 *Julia Child & More Company*

PAGES 29, 35, 51, 65, AND 85 *The Way to Cook*

PAGES 41, 49, 102, 111, AND 131 *Julia Child & Company*

PAGES 45, 90, 103, 105, 125, AND 141 *Mastering the Art of French Cooking, Volume II* (with Simone Beck)

PAGE 101 *The French Chef Cookbook*

OTHER SOURCES

PAGES 13, 36, AND 99 *Good Morning America*

PAGES 17 AND 46 *Backstage with Julia: My Years with Julia Child* by Nancy Verde Barr

PAGE 23 *Gastronomica: The Journal of Critical Food Studies* ("A Conversation with Julia Child, Spring 1984" by Sharon Hudgins, vol. 5, no. 3, Summer 2005)

PAGES 31, 57, 73, AND 117 *As Always, Julia: The Letters of Julia Child & Avis DeVoto* (edited by Joan Reardon)

PAGES 25, 47, 62, AND 121 *Interview* magazine ("Julia Child" by Polly Frost, August 1989)

PAGE 55 Letter to Avis DeVoto (January 5, 1971)

PAGE 69 Associated Press ("Learn to Cook with 'Gusto' Advises Kitchen's Grand Dame," September 27, 1978)

PAGES 75 AND 79 *Esquire* (June 2000)

PAGE 81 *The Interviews: An Oral History of Television* (interview with Michael Rosen, Television Academy Foundation, June 25, 1999, edited by Adrienne Faillace)

PAGE 91 *The French Chef* (WGBH Public Television)

PAGES 95 AND 113 *Particular Passions: Talks with Women Who Have Shaped Our Times* by Lynn Gilbert

PAGE 127 *The French Chef in America* by Alex Prud'homme

PAGE 129 *Appetite for Life: The Biography of Julia Child* by Noël Riley Fitch

PAGES 11, 33, 43, 61, 77, 89, AND 133 verified by The Julia Child Foundation for Gastronomy and the Culinary Arts

A NOTE ABOUT THE AUTHOR

Julia Child was born in Pasadena, California, in 1912. She graduated from Smith College and worked for the OSS during World War II. She married Paul Child and they moved to Paris, where she studied at the Cordon Bleu. In Paris, she taught cooking with Simone Beck and Louisette Bertholle, with whom she wrote the first volume of *Mastering the Art of French Cooking* (1961). In 1963, Boston's WGBH launched *The French Chef* television series, which made Julia Child a national celebrity, earning her the Peabody Award in 1964 and an Emmy in 1966, the first of several. After a more than fifty year career as an author, teacher, and advocate for home cooking, including numerous public television series and best-selling cookbooks, she remains a beloved culinary icon. In 2002, her Cambridge, Massachusetts, kitchen, featured in many of her television series, was displayed at the Smithsonian's National Museum of American History, where it now anchors the museum's first major exhibit on food history. She was awarded the French Legion of Honor in 2000 and the U.S. Presidential Medal of Freedom in 2003 for her contributions to French and American culture. She died in Santa Barbara, California, in 2004, two days before her ninety-second birthday. Since then, The Julia Child Foundation for Gastronomy and the Culinary Arts, which Julia established before she died, has continued her legacy, by educating and encouraging others to cook, eat, and drink well, through grants and by presenting the annual Julia Child Award.

A NOTE ON THE TYPE

The text of this book was set in Filosofia, a typeface designed by Zuzana Licko in 1996 as a revival of the typefaces of Giambattista Bodoni (1740–1813). Basing her design on the letterpress practice of altering the cut of the letters to match the size for which they were to be used, Licko designed Filosofia Regular as a rugged face with reduced contrast to withstand the reduction to text sizes, and Filosofia Grand as a more delicate and refined version for use in larger display sizes.

Composed by North Market Street Graphics
Lancaster, Pennsylvania

Printed and bound by Friesens Corporation
Altona, Canada